Nine Fundamentals of Golf That Will Improve Your Marriage

The Front Nine

Roger and Becky Tirabassi

HOWARD
PUBLISHING CO.

ROGER AND BECKY TIRABASSI have been married more than twenty-five years in a partnership that works to change people's lives and are the coauthors of *Let Love Change Your Life*. Roger is a professional counselor to married and engaged couples, with an M.A. from Bowling Green State University. He is a certified sports counselor and member of SCGA. Becky is a nationally acclaimed motivational speaker, best-selling author of *Change Your Life*, and president of Becky Tirabassi Change Your Life, Inc., a multimedia company that encourages balanced living through published resources, television, radio, and events. Becky is ACE certified and a member of EWGA, Women's SCGA, and USGA.

RICK HUNTER, serving as consultant on this book, is a PGA Member, a teaching professional, an Associate Member of the Senior PGA Tour, 2000 Southern California Senior PGA Match Play champion, and 2001 Southern California Senior PGA Chapter Champion.

TO CONTACT the Tirabassis to speak at a couples conference or to host a *Front Nine* event, please call, e-mail, or write them at:

800-444-6189

www.thefrontnine.com

cyl@changeyourlifedaily.com

Change Your Life

Box 9672

Newport Beach, CA 92660

The Front Nine © 2003 by Roger and Becky Tirabassi
All rights reserved. Printed in the United States of America

Published by Howard Publishing Co., Inc.
3117 North 7th Street, West Monroe, Louisiana 71291-2227

03 04 05 06 07 08 09 10 11 12   10 9 8 7 6 5 4 3 2 1

Edited by Between the Lines
Cover and interior design by LinDee Loveland
Photography of Becky and Roger Tirabassi by Figge Photography,
    taken at Strawberry Farms Golf Club
    11 Strawberry Farms Rd.
    Irvine, CA 92612
    www.strawberryfarmsgolf.com

ISBN: 1-58229-292-2

Contents

Golf and Marriage: Discover the Links   *1*

Fundamental #1:   Loosen Your Grip   *7*

Fundamental #2:   Master Many Skills   *15*

Fundamental #3:   Maintain a Positive Attitude   *25*

Fundamental #4:   What Feels Natural Isn't Always Best   *35*

Fundamental #5:   Repair Divots Immediately   *43*

Fundamental #6:   Getting Better Takes Time and Practice   *51*

Fundamental #7:   Avoid the Hazards   *59*

Fundamental #8:   Have Realistic Expectations   *71*

Fundamental #9:   When in a Slump, Get Back to Basics   *79*

Rounding the Turn: Great Players Take Lessons   *87*

GOLF AND MARRIAGE
Discover the Links

Golf is a lot like marriage! Once you venture into either, you'll find it to be emotionally thrilling—and difficult. Each is very time-consuming and requires that you know how to control your emotions, master many fundamentals, and get out of trouble quickly!

Whether on the golf course or at home, sometimes it takes only one bad shot to turn fun into frustration. Early on, we made a commitment to enjoy our marriage and the game of golf for a lifetime. After twenty-five years together, we're happy to report that on the golf course and in marriage, we still find enjoyment. We've also discovered that many fundamental rules of golf also apply in marriage. Yes, golf can help you improve your relationship!

The Front Nine: Nine Fundamentals of Golf That Will Improve Your Marriage is a compilation of straightforward advice from the experts. Roger is a certified marriage counselor, and both of us are avid golfers.

1

Golf and Marriage

Becky's brother, Rick Hunter, is a PGA member, instructor, tournament player, and consultant for this book.

Our golf history begins even before we were born. Becky's father worked as a caddie in the 1920s. By the early 1940s, his love for the game had propelled him to the position of golf course superintendent at a beautiful Cleveland, Ohio, country club. Becky's mother learned to play golf when her 1939 high school physical education teacher took students to a municipal golf course for lessons. After Becky's parents met and married in 1942, they traveled with other couples to Turkey Foot Golf Course in Akron, Ohio, where the women picnicked and the men played golf. After only a few picnics, Becky's mother determined that she would rather golf. Soon she was playing regularly, and she continues weekly league and recreational golf today, sixty years later! Together, the Hunters enjoyed golf and marriage for more than fifty years.

Becky has golfed for most of her life. She golfs regularly with her mom, husband, brother, and son. She also is the unabashed recipient of free marriage counseling from her husband and expert golf instruction from her brother.

Discover the Links

Roger's story begins at the age of five, when his dad took him to a golf course called "the cow pasture." (It was a cow pasture before it became a golf course and, even after the transformation, it never looked much different.) Roger's father let him walk the course carrying a pitching wedge, using it for every shot from tee to green. To this day, Roger contends that the pitching wedge is the best club in his bag.

Roger's dad taught him that golf was a game he could enjoy his entire life. He also showed Roger that marriage could be enjoyed for a lifetime. Roger Sr. played golf until the last year of his life, and his marriage lasted fifty-nine years, until his death.

The nine fundamentals in this book are ones we apply both on the golf course and in our home. Doing so brings us joy, confidence, and pleasure whether we're on a coastal resort or in "the cow pasture." Our hope is that this book will help you not only improve your marriage but take a few strokes off your golf game as well.

Discover the Links

I'm not a believer in "methods."
I am a believer in fundamentals.

Jack Nicklaus

from *Golf My Way*

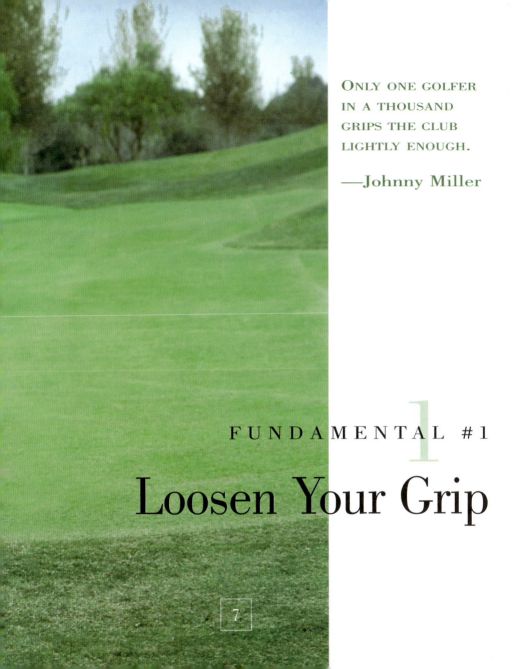

ONLY ONE GOLFER
IN A THOUSAND
GRIPS THE CLUB
LIGHTLY ENOUGH.

—Johnny Miller

FUNDAMENTAL #1

Loosen Your Grip

Loosen Your Grip

George Knudson was a legend among golf pros and a student of the golf swing. Ben Hogan, golf legend of the 1940s and 50s, said Knudson had the best swing of his generation.

In his book *The Natural Golf Swing,* Knudson tells how he initially tried to develop a tight golf grip, believing it would produce a stable club face. Instead, he determined—over time and after a great deal of hard work—that the most natural and powerful golf swing could be achieved by holding the club lightly enough to barely feel the grip against the skin of your hands.

Surprised by his own discovery, Knudson wrote, "Now I stand up to the ball and I feel as if I'm hardly holding on to the club. That's freedom. That's balance. Then I just let the club face go where it will. But in those days I didn't understand these things. I was still controlling. I was still holding on with my mind and my body. I didn't know how to relax, and that was sad. This is the fear of losing control. It comes from a lack of understanding."

Every golfer would be wise to take this advice to the course. Those of us who have held on to a golf club too tightly know from experience that this can cause several undesirable results: loss of distance, slower club head speed, and a ball that is apt to fly in the wrong direction. Though it seems that a tight grip would bring more power and control, it usually produces a shorter drive.

When you loosen your grip, your swing becomes more natural and relaxed, the club head goes naturally into proper positions, and you'll experience every golfer's dream—unrestrained freedom and balance.

THOUGH IT SEEMS THAT A **TIGHT** GRIP WOULD BRING **MORE** POWER AND CONTROL, IT USUALLY **PRODUCES** A SHORTER DRIVE.

Loosen Your Grip

One of the most common criticisms Roger hears in his counseling office is, "My spouse is so controlling! He (or she) tells me how to drive, cook, what to say, and what not to say! It drives me crazy!"

When we tighten our grip or try to "control" a spouse, it has the same effect as when we tighten our grip on a golf club. By criticizing, micromanaging, or failing to make allowances for our differing personalities, we put undue tension and pressure on the relationship, and we won't get the results we want—freedom and balance.

A "loose grip" in marriage can mean eliminating critical comments or refraining from asserting your preferred style into your spouse's method of doing things.

Usually husbands and wives don't realize that their behavior feels controlling to their spouse. They think they're just being helpful.

A "loose grip" in marriage can mean eliminating critical comments or refraining from asserting your preferred style into your spouse's method of doing things. As you see the freedom that comes with a loosened grip, you'll be encouraged and motivated to let your spouse develop strengths, pursue dreams, and overcome obstacles!

Loosening your grip is a matter of paying close attention to your spouse's personality and strengths and of being an encourager rather than tightening the grip of control that can squelch a healthy relationship.

grip

1. the delicate balance between freedom and "have and hold" in relation to your spouse

2. the way one holds a golf club; the fine balance between loose and firm hands appropriately placed for maximum distance and accuracy

Loosen Your Grip

Golf is a target game, and we should direct all our
efforts toward making a swing motion toward the
target while letting our bodies travel freely.

George Knudson

from *The Natural Golf Swing*

I BUILD CONFIDENCE
WHEN I PRACTICE A
VARIETY OF SHOTS—
HITTING IT HIGH
OR LOW, WORKING
THE BALL. MY
CONFIDENCE IS
BUILT ON KNOWING
I CAN EFFECTIVELY
WORK THE
BALL IN ANY
CIRCUMSTANCE.

—JoAnne Carner

FUNDAMENTAL #2

Master Many Skills

Master Many Skills

Golf is one of the most challenging sports for a person to learn because a golfer has to master many different shots with a variety of clubs—putt with a putter, chip and pitch with wedges and short irons, and execute a full swing with long irons, fairway metals, and a driver.

But that's not all! As soon as you become skilled with various clubs, you must begin to factor in the elements—such as wind, slope of the fairways and greens, speed of the greens, and distance—for every shot.

Inexperienced golfers often underestimate how important *every* shot on the course is to the overall score. Beginners are notorious for focusing on a powerful drive, forgetting that whether it's a two-hundred-yard drive or a two-foot putt, it's still one stroke on the scorecard.

Eventually, a plateau in score or repeated failure in one aspect of the game will force a player to concentrate on improving his or her weaknesses. Sooner or later, players realize that understanding course management, the role of every club in the bag, and how to factor in the elements that impact a round of golf are critical to a better score and a more enjoyable experience.

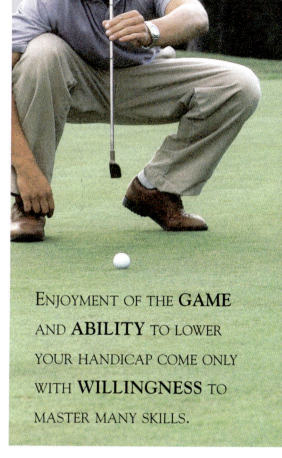

Seasoned golfers are acutely aware that every round of golf—even every shot—will challenge them. But they also know that enjoyment of the game and the ability to lower your handicap come only with willingness to master many skills.

ENJOYMENT OF THE **GAME** AND **ABILITY** TO LOWER YOUR HANDICAP COME ONLY WITH **WILLINGNESS** TO MASTER MANY SKILLS.

Golf is a passive game, one in which we let most things happen rather than make them happen.

GEORGE KNUDSON

from *The Natural Golf Swing*

Master Many Skills

Roger counsels many men who can't understand why their wives are unhappy. They'll say things like, "I've been married for six years. I bring home a paycheck every week, and my wife has enough money to buy almost anything she wants. She has a nice car and beautiful clothes and lives in one of the nicest suburbs in the area. What does it take to make a woman happy these days?" These husbands feel their wives are too demanding and unappreciative. The men contend that no matter what they do, it isn't enough.

Then their wives join them for a session and share their

Often couples don't realize how many skills are required to build and enjoy a healthy marriage for a lifetime.

18

feelings about the marriage. Their remarks sound something like this: "I have a beautiful home, but I'm not happy. My husband is a great provider who works very hard. In fact, he works too hard. He comes home late almost every night. He plays golf nearly every Saturday, but he's too tired to talk, too tired to help me around the house, and not very affectionate except when he wants to have sex."

Often couples underestimate how much effort it takes to sustain a good relationship. They don't realize how many skills are required to build and enjoy a healthy marriage for a lifetime.

Roger suggests that couples learn a specific set of marriage skills. In addition to helping couples learn to give encouragement and take a good dose of humility, he teaches them the "14 Rules for Effective Communication" found in our book *Let Love Change Your Life*:

1. Don't use the words "never" and "always."
2. Don't blame, shame, or call names.
3. Use "I" statements rather than "you" statements.
4. Say "I am hurt" rather than "I am angry or mad."
5. Take a time-out.

6. Don't withdraw or isolate.
7. Repeat to the person what he or she said to you before you share your thoughts, feelings, or possible solutions.
8. Don't interrupt.
9. Don't demand.
10. Use the phrase "I would like" rather than "I need."
11. Don't use threats.
12. Be affirming.
13. Never use the D word (divorce).
14. Don't use the statement "You broke a rule."

Mastery of these and other communication skills, such as anger management and conflict resolution, will lead to a more satisfying marriage and a lifetime of having fun, growing in love, and staying committed to each other.

Marriage is like twirling a baton, turning handsprings, or eating with chopsticks. It looks so easy till you try it.
HELEN ROWLAND

ready play

1. an easygoing, not overly critical approach to marriage; not overanalyzing situations; moving along in communication with your spouse without belaboring points and problems

2. a casual or friendly format of play in which the golfer who is most ready to hit a ball does so; allows a quicker pace of play on the course

etiquette

1. kind, polite things you do for your spouse that show appreciation and affection, keeping the relationship fun

2. an extensive list of suggested behaviors that ensure politeness and good manners on the golf course, making the game more enjoyable for everyone

Master Many Skills

The important thing is to be prepared for both bad shots and the bad breaks the course can dish out even on good shots.

Bob Rotella

from *Golf Is Not a Game of Perfect*

THE WINNERS ARE
THE ONES WHO ARE
THINKING THE BEST,
USING THEIR MINDS
THE BEST.

—Nancy Lopez

FUNDAMENTAL **3** #3

Maintain a
Positive Attitude

Maintain a Positive Attitude

Becky recently read *Golf Is Not a Game of Perfect,* by Dr. Bob Rotella, which focuses on the mental, rather than the physical, aspect of the sport. One of Dr. Rotella's main themes is, "Negative thinking is almost 100 percent effective." He doesn't want golfers to even entertain thoughts like, *I'll bet I'm going to hit into that huge sand trap* or, *Oh no, a water hazard. I always find a way to hit into them.* Why? Because those who dwell on the possibility of landing in the water and sand—or who look right at the hazard—focus more on the hazard than on the fairway. The result is, they end up in the hazard almost 100 percent of the time!

Harvey Penick, instructor and author of *The Little Red Book,* agrees. He says, "When it comes to hitting a golf shot, a negative thought is pure poison."

On the golf course it's important to hold on to positive, focused thoughts, especially when you land in a hazard or behind a tree. By staying calm and positive, you give yourself a greater chance of making a better shot.

Becky applied this principle to her game recently. The others in her regular foursome (Roger, Rick, and Becky's mom) watched in amazement as Becky's ball landed on the green, just two feet from the cup, in only four shots on a long, par-five hole. They all held their breath as Becky proceeded to…miss the putt for a bogey. They waited for her reaction to this critical putt. She looked up and sighed—and then smiled! When they realized that she wasn't devastated, ashamed, or angry over the miss, they relaxed and shared sympathetic laughter.

Becky resolved not to let the missed putt have a negative effect on her disposition. She had to shake off the effects of such an unfortunate miss and maintain a positive attitude.

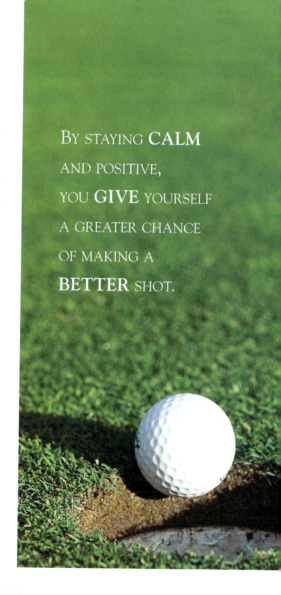

BY STAYING **CALM** AND POSITIVE, YOU **GIVE** YOURSELF A GREATER CHANCE OF MAKING A **BETTER** SHOT.

Maintain a Positive Attitude

On the next hole, a par four, she was on the green in two shots, but with more than fifty feet left to the hole. Could she make the long putt for a birdie? If she thought about her last two-foot putt, she would feel the odds were against her. But she was determined to go for it, believing she could make the shot. As the ball headed toward the hole at a perfect speed and line, the players held their breath. When the ball went in the hole for a birdie, Becky lay flat out on the green, and they all celebrated with joyful laughter.

Try this: Talk kindly and positively to yourself after a bad shot. Watch your score improve and the level of your enjoyment for the game increase!

Rule your mind or it will rule you.
HORACE

birdie

1. pet name you use for your wife when she does something special or sweet for you

2. one stroke under par on a hole, meaning you played a great hole!

slice

1. an errant action, comment, or facial expression that causes immediate friction between marriage partners; usually needs correction and can cause unwanted results in the relationship

2. an errant shot that often misses the fairway or green; usually needs correction and can cause an unwanted increase in score

Maintain a Positive Attitude

In marriage, there are ample opportunities for couples to hit rough spots. A poorly timed or sarcastic comment, selfish behavior, or even a simple misunderstanding can steal a light-hearted moment or ruin a fabulous day. How can we maintain a positive attitude on a daily basis in our marriage? Withholding critical statements and disapproving looks and responding to a negative or vulnerable situation with encouraging remarks and empathy will help us get through those inevitable rough spots more quickly.

Think about how you would react at a golf outing when a

A simple adjustment in your attitude at home will do as much or more good as it does on the golf course.

negative situation unfolded. You would exercise self-control and try to display your best attitude. You might not "win" the moment, but you would retain respect and allow common courtesy to walk you through an uncomfortable or unfortunate situation.

Now transfer that discipline into your marriage. Don't let your spouse be the first to see your attitude lose its luster. A simple adjustment in your attitude at home will do as much or more good as it does on the golf course.

Maintaining a positive attitude in your marriage will promote mutual respect. All marriages hit rough spots. But when we treat each other with respect and willingness to forgive quickly, rather than trying to "win" or rub in the other person's mistake, we'll elicit a lot more laughter than tears or silence. If you desire a fun, successful marriage, maintaining a positive attitude is the only option!

Whatever is true, whatever is noble, whatever is right,
whatever is pure, whatever is lovely, whatever is admirable—
if anything is excellent or praiseworthy—think about such things.
PHILIPPIANS 4:8

31

Maintain a Positive Attitude

You have to put your expectations out of your
mind by the time you get to the first tee.

Bob Rotella

from *Golf Is Not a Game of Perfect*

THERE IS NOTHING
NATURAL ABOUT
THE GOLF SWING.

—Ben Hogan

FUNDAMENTAL #4

What Feels Natural
Isn't Always Best

What Feels Natural Isn't Always Best

Upon entering a benefit golf tournament, Roger welcomed the advice of a visiting golf professional watching him struggle on the practice tee. The instructor focused on changing Roger's grip. He suggested that Roger's left hand was turned a little too far to the left. He instructed him to wrap both his right hand and left hand to form a V between his thumb and forefinger, both Vs pointing toward his right shoulder.

That grip felt unnatural to Roger, and he commented, "There's no way I'll be able to hit the ball like this. It feels terrible!"

The pro smiled and said, "Just give it a try." To Roger's surprise, the ball shot powerfully off the club face and straight out into the range with a desirable slight draw. It was a great shot. "How did that feel?" the pro asked Roger.

"It felt terrible," Roger replied, "but I love the results!"

The pro smiled again. "Just keep doing what feels unnatural until it starts to feel natural," he advised.

Changing a stance, grip, or swing—especially if you've gotten into a rut or a bad habit or never learned correctly—isn't easy. It will be uncomfortable and feel unnatural at first. It takes time to change

JUST KEEP **DOING** WHAT **FEELS** UNNATURAL UNTIL IT STARTS TO FEEL **NATURAL.**

your muscle memory, to unlearn old patterns and replace them with new ones. But if you want to improve your golf game, you must be willing to change.

whiff

1. a forgotten birthday, anniversary, or special event; usually costs a spouse some effort to compensate
2. a swing and a miss; costs a golf player one stroke

What Feels Natural Isn't Always Best

Putting new habits into practice in your marriage might bring discomfort, but it will also yield greater results and consistent improvement.

In a marriage relationship, changing poor habits and learning new, more effective practices is difficult—the new skills don't feel natural, even when they seem as "basic" as listening.

One of the most effective techniques Roger teaches couples is called *intentional listening* (also known as active listening or mirroring). Each person must listen and then repeat the thoughts and feelings expressed by his or her spouse. The listening spouse then must empathize with those thoughts and feelings before sharing his or her own.

Though this is an effective pattern for healthy communica-

38

tion, couples find it uncomfortable and difficult to incorporate this practice into their daily lives. Nevertheless, Roger asks them to practice this proven system, knowing that it will lead to desired results: improvement in their relationship.

Roger encourages couples to try this method of communication in front of him. He carefully coaches them, stopping them from speaking before they've first repeated what the other person said. Then he walks them through the process of repeating their partner's thoughts and feelings and helps move them into empathy for each other. Though most couples report that using this communication style initially feels unnatural, even mechanical, they also agree that their increased level of intimacy is worth the learning curve.

Continually adapting and learning new and better skills must be a lifelong commitment for those who desire to improve their relationships. What feels natural isn't always best. Putting new habits into practice in your marriage might bring discomfort, but it will also yield greater results and consistent improvement.

God made what is called the lifeline in the right
palm of a human being for one very special
reason.…It fits just exactly perfectly against
the left thumb in a good golf grip.

Harvey Penick

from *And If You Play Golf, You're My Friend*

41

I AM REPLACING
ALL THE GRASS I
DUG UP WHEN
I WAS ON THE TOUR.

—Marlene Hagge,
on gardening in
her retirement

FUNDAMENTAL 5 #5

Repair Divots Immediately

Repair Divots Immediately

Golf is a unique sport of rules and etiquette. Repairing divots is part of that etiquette. Those who teach or play golf for a living have a motto: Leave the golf course in better condition than when you arrived. If you golf, you will make divots. It's part of the game. But unrepaired divots can hinder play.

For example, if you land in a divot on the course, you're not allowed to pick your ball out of the hole. Because of a previous player's failure to repair his or her divot, your difficulty is increased. Ultimately, your score can be negatively affected by the inconsideration of one who does not immediately repair the damage caused by his or her play.

Signs posted on the course and often in the carts, as well as in golf handbooks, explain the importance of immediate attention to even the smallest marring of the course: "It takes five seconds to fix a divot. An immediately repaired divot or ball mark takes one to two days to heal. If you wait an hour to repair, it takes two weeks to heal. Unrepaired ball marks take three weeks to properly heal, leaving unsightly, uneven putting surfaces."

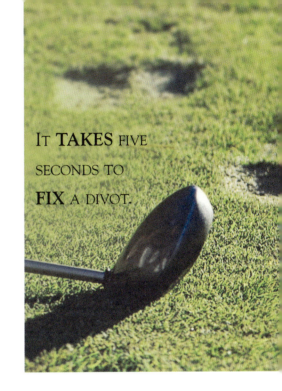

Repairing divots immediately minimizes damage to the course and makes the game more enjoyable for everyone.

IT **TAKES** FIVE SECONDS TO **FIX** A DIVOT.

glossary

divot

1. a hurtful comment or inconsideration that requires a quick apology to keep your relationship happy and healthy

2. a chunk of grass taken out of the playing surface by the swing of a club; if not repaired immediately, it will take longer to heal, and its mark could negatively affect the play of others

Repair Divots Immediately

The principle of quickly repairing divots on the golf course can easily translate into quickly making amends in your marriage. It's inevitable that you will hurt and be hurt by your spouse. But much like the timely repairing of a divot on the golf course affects the quality of the course, how quickly you attempt to repair and address hurts will determine the condition of your marriage.

The sooner we ask for forgiveness after hurting someone, the easier it is to move forward together. The longer we wait to reconcile our differences, the more difficult it becomes to

The longer we wait to reconcile our differences, the more difficult it becomes to resolve them.

resolve them. In fact, the longer we wait to resolve conflict, the greater the chance additional trouble will enter the relationship and complicate our lives even more.

The Bible says, "Do not let the sun go down while you are still angry" (Ephesians 4:26). It encourages us not to let a day go by without taking care of the hurt we might have caused another. Just as there's good reason to quickly repair divots on the golf course, there's a vital reason to quickly repair divots in our relationships: faster healing!

Over the years, we've developed a plan to deal quickly with conflict. As soon as we realize we've hurt or offended each other, we offer words that we know will melt away our defenses: "Will you forgive me?" Forgiveness comes more easily when you remember that, probably sooner than later, you'll be the one in need of forgiveness!

On the golf course and in your marriage, be committed to repairing divots and resolving conflicts immediately. It will make your marriage healthier and your life together more enjoyable!

Do not let the sun go down while you are still angry.
EPHESIANS 4:26

Repair Divots Immediately

In our play, we reveal what
kind of people we are.

Ovid

GOLF IS A SCIENCE, THE STUDY OF A LIFETIME, IN WHICH YOU CAN EXHAUST YOURSELF BUT NEVER YOUR SUBJECT.

—David Forgan

FUNDAMENTAL #6

Getting Better Takes Time and Practice

Getting Better Takes Time and Practice

A great golf swing can be achieved through a variety of means: golf lessons, better equipment, time on the practice tee, and playing golf on a regular basis. Though most golfers admit that they want a great swing, they often won't spend the time it takes to achieve one. Harvey Penick, one of golf's greatest instructors, said, "Lessons are not to take the place of practice but to make practice worthwhile."

The temptation for beginning golfers is to observe how effortlessly pros hit the ball and to naively think they should be able to perform the same way without the same investment. They forget or don't realize that professional golfers can be found on the practice tee or golf course day after day after day—driving, chipping, hitting sand shots, and putting.

Phil Mickelson's practice routine includes hitting four-foot putts until he makes ten in a row. Sometimes he hits a hundred putts before he completes this regimen. Though this exercise costs him considerable time, it provides him with great confidence and success in competitive matches.

Excellence on the golf course comes only with a considerable amount of practice and playing time. Rick Hunter echoes the wisdom of countless other PGA instructors when he reminds us, "There are no shortcuts to improvement in the game of golf."

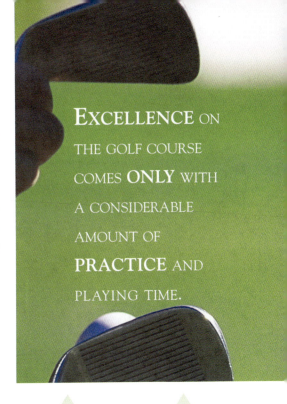

EXCELLENCE ON THE GOLF COURSE COMES ONLY WITH A CONSIDERABLE AMOUNT OF PRACTICE AND PLAYING TIME.

mulligan

1. overlooking a bad choice (e.g., critical or hurtful comment, inconsiderate action, or oversight) by your spouse

2. overlooking a bad shot and not counting it, as though it didn't happen; not an acceptable practice in handicap or tournament play, but welcome among friends!

Getting Better Takes Time and Practice

Maintaining a healthy and happy marriage takes time and effort. But practicing good communication skills is the key to keeping your marriage on course.

Success in marriage is no different. It takes quality and quantity time together to enjoy a great relationship with your spouse. Yet one of the most common complaints Roger hears men share is, "My wife wants to talk all the time. She wants to know all about my day." He smiles every time he hears those words…and then he instructs couples to set aside specific times to talk. It takes practice to get better at communicating, and setting aside a special time is helpful, especially if you have an ongoing conflict.

In our own relationship, we recently experienced a few days

54

when everything we said seemed to bounce right off each other. We weren't connecting. In fact, we were only irritating each other. And you know how that goes—each irritation seems to build on the one before, and the next thing you know, you're either speaking to each other harshly or not at all.

Finally, Becky broke the ice when she suggested, "I think we need to make an appointment to talk." We determined that at 7:30 that evening we would sit down and practice our communication skills. We pulled out our book *Let Love Change Your Life* and went through each step of the intentional listening and conflict resolution methods. In about twenty minutes, we were back in sync—and both convinced that we would have carried on like two children for days had we not taken time to practice our relationship skills.

Maintaining a healthy and happy marriage takes time and effort. Practicing good communication skills is the key to keeping your marriage on course.

Married life offers no panacea—if it is going to reach its potential, it will require an all-out investment by both husband and wife.
JAMES DOBSON

Getting

er Takes Time and Practice

To improve, you must practice. But the quality of
your practice is more important than the quantity.

Bob Rotella

from *Golf Is Not a Game of Perfect*

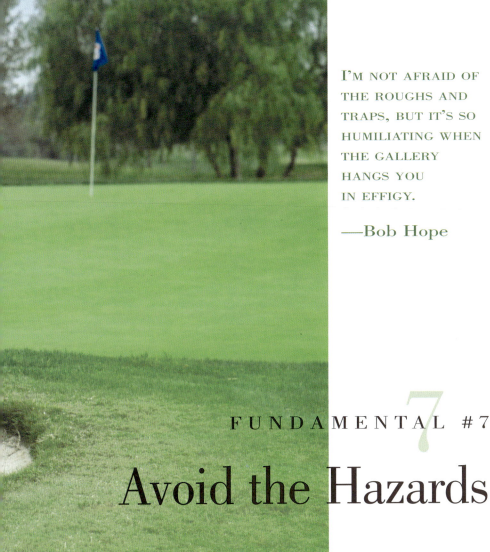

I'M NOT AFRAID OF
THE ROUGHS AND
TRAPS, BUT IT'S SO
HUMILIATING WHEN
THE GALLERY
HANGS YOU
IN EFFIGY.

—Bob Hope

FUNDAMENTAL #7

Avoid the Hazards

Avoid the Hazards

Sand traps, water hazards, out-of-bounds markers, and a forest of trees all have the potential to ruin a great day for many golfers. Some hazards are hidden—until you are in them. Others are foreseeable, and the wise golfer will avoid them.

Rick Hunter advises, "A good golfer has to have a plan or a strategy for avoiding hazards. The best way to do this is to make note of the hazards on a particular hole or course and play it safe whenever you're near or around them." This is a great idea—but it takes quite a bit of self-control to accomplish!

Case in point: On a golf course where we often play, a relatively short par-three hole has a lake running from the right side of the tee box all the way to the back of the green. The flag is usually placed on the right portion of the green, fifteen feet from the edge, just next to the water. Roger is convinced this pin placement is to tempt idealistic golfers like him. Almost every time he comes to this hole, he thinks, *I can birdie this hole if I just aim right for the pin!* He's especially vulnerable to this temptation if he's been hitting the ball fairly straight. He ignores the water hazard and aims straight for the pin.

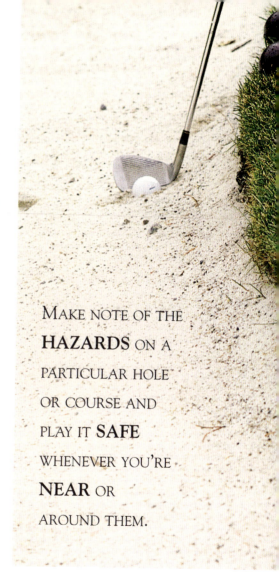

It almost doesn't matter how well Roger is hitting that day. On this short hole, something always happens. He'll either fade the ball or, worse, hit a full-blown slice. Either way, he's in the water for a certain double bogey.

Over and over, he thinks that this time the water hazard won't get him.

Finally, after numerous double bogeys, Roger has determined to ignore his aspirations for a birdie, stay calm, and aim for the safer, left side of the green. This strategy almost always assures him of a par or at least a bogey. Most important, when he follows this plan, he rarely gets a double bogey.

MAKE NOTE OF THE **HAZARDS** ON A PARTICULAR HOLE OR COURSE AND PLAY IT **SAFE** WHENEVER YOU'RE **NEAR** OR AROUND THEM.

Avoid the Hazards

Rick's advice concerning hazards is "Know where the hazards are, then focus totally on your target. Remember, your exact target may not be the pin. Your strategy might include aiming left, right, short of, or beyond the pin placement."

Of course, if you are in a hazard, calmly assess your best chance of minimizing additional strokes. Proper club selection, course management, and a positive attitude will help you do this. But having a good strategy in place to avoid the hazards can be the key to a better overall score and a more enjoyable game.

There is no such thing as a misplaced bunker. Regardless of where a bunker may be, it is the business of a player to avoid it.
DONALD ROSS

hazard

1. a place of trouble for couples (e.g., a sore topic, unwelcome comment, or certain "look") that is known for causing disruption in positive communication

2. a place of trouble (e.g., water, sand trap, tree, or out-of-bounds marker) that adds penalties to a golfer's score

gimme

1. extending grace and mercy after a hurtful remark or irritation

2. when your playing partner allows you to pick up the ball on the green, rather than requiring you to finish the putt

Avoid the Hazards

Make a list of the specific hazards that have caused "double bogeys" in the course of your marriage and consider them out of bounds.

After twenty-five years of marriage, we've learned that just as there are hazards to avoid in golf, so there are "hazards" to avoid in marriage. Giving unsolicited advice can be one of them!

One recent Father's Day, we went out late in the afternoon to play eighteen holes. Becky wasn't excited about playing—she had been struggling with her game, slicing the ball—but she was willing to go because she knew Roger wanted to play. Because Roger wanted her to do well, when she sliced the ball for the fifth time, he suggested that she either try to swing a little more inside out or just play the slice by aiming to the left. She took his advice, and the next ball went perfectly straight…into a lake.

Not only was Becky mad about losing the stroke (she counts all penalties and whiffs, and there are no mulligans in her game), she was irritated with Roger for telling her how to hit the ball. On top of that, she was sure it was his advice that caused her to second-guess her shot and send her favorite ball, the Lady Precept, into a water hazard.

Author Harvey Penick cautions couples against unsolicited advice: "No pretty woman can take a single shot without a man giving her some poor advice."

Here are some common hazards to avoid in your marriage:

- Monopolizing the television remote control
- Criticizing in-laws
- Repeatedly keeping each other waiting
- Forgetting birthdays, anniversaries, or anything important to your spouse
- Telling your spouse how to drive or do some simple task
- Disapproving of your spouse's club selection

Avoid the Hazards

Both of us have hit into the above hazards more times than we can count. Each time we're tempted to think, *This time it will be OK to bring this up,* we end up with a double or triple bogey! We temporarily lose the fun in our friendship and have to work hard to recover it.

We suggest that you have a strategy for avoiding the hazards in your relationship. Make a list of the specific hazards that have caused "double bogeys" in the course of your marriage and consider them out of bounds. Do your best to stay clear of them. It will help you experience a safer and more enjoyable relationship with both immediate and long-term rewards.

He who covers over an offense promotes love, but whoever repeats the matter separates close friends.
PROVERBS 17:9

fairway

1. the best way to achieve a win-win situation in your relationship

2. the surface running from tee to green that is a golfer's target in order to find the best lie, angle, and placement for his or her next shot(s) on the way to the green

flex

1. the important "give" ingredient in the fine art of negotiation and communication

2. the amount of bend in the shaft of a golf club

Avoid the Hazards

Course management includes knowing
when to go for it and when to lay up.

Tiger Woods

from *How I Play Golf*

HIT THE SHOT YOU
KNOW YOU CAN
HIT, NOT THE SHOT
ARNOLD PALMER
WOULD HIT, NOR
EVEN THE SHOT
YOU THINK YOU
SHOULD BE ABLE
TO HIT.

—Bob Rotella

FUNDAMENTAL #8

Have Realistic
Expectations

Have Realistic Expectations

We spend quite a few hours watching the PGA, Senior PGA, and LPGA golf tournaments on television. We marvel at how simple these professionals make the game of golf appear! We are amazed at the way they can launch a ball two hundred yards with their five-irons when neither of us can hit a ball that far with our five-woods. But by the end of the tournament, we start believing we have the potential to be that good someday.

It's the tendency of every golfer to think he or she can play like the pros and hit excellent shots consistently. But most books and magazine articles about golf report this reality: In any given round, the average recreational golfer can expect to hit only a few great shots.

For pros and amateurs alike, one of the keys to enjoying golf is to expect to hit some poor shots. The key is to not dwell on them—or the results can be devastating. If you let a poor lie or a bad shot consume you, it will steal your focus and take the fun out of the game for you and those around you.

What is a realistic expectation for the average golfer who approaches the first tee? Acknowledge the nuances of the game, enjoy your companions and the beauty of the course, and play your round one shot at a time. Of course, your personality, level of intensity, and competitiveness will factor into the way you golf. But having realistic expectations gives everyone the opportunity for a more enjoyable experience on the course.

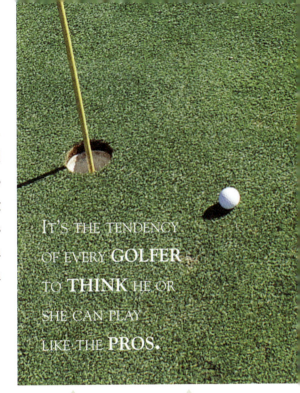

IT'S THE TENDENCY OF EVERY **GOLFER** TO **THINK** HE OR SHE CAN PLAY LIKE THE **PROS.**

bogey

1. something you did to cause a little difficulty in the course of your marriage
2. one stroke over par, meaning you had a little difficulty with the hole

Have Realistic Expectations

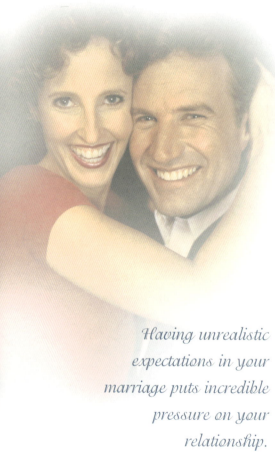

Just as having unrealistic expectations on the golf course puts a strain on your game, having unrealistic expectations in your marriage puts incredible pressure on your relationship. No matter how hard you try, your marriage will not be perfect or without conflict.

Roger has seen through his practice that couples who expect their marriages to always run smoothly often are devastated when they encounter trouble. Rather than quickly resolving their disagreements by using practical methods for conflict resolution and anger management, they are inclined to over-

Having unrealistic expectations in your marriage puts incredible pressure on your relationship.

react to the problem. And because the conflicts are unexpected, these couples are easily discouraged.

Often couples come into the counseling office expecting that after three sessions their conflicts will be resolved and their marriage will succeed without further effort. Roger reminds these couples to be realistic. Successful marriages take time, effort, and understanding. Just as expecting your handicap to drop ten strokes after three or four lessons with a golf instructor is unrealistic, so is expecting rapid improvement in a troubled relationship.

What are your expectations of your spouse and of your marriage? If you are realistic, optimistic, and patient with yourself and with your partner, we are convinced that—over time—your marriage will improve!

A happy marriage is the union of two good forgivers.
ROBERT QUILLEN

Have Realistic Expectations

Golf is all about recovering
from bad shots.

Bob Rotella

from *Golf Is Not a Game of Perfect*

IF YOU PLAY
POORLY ONE DAY,
FORGET IT. IF YOU
PLAY POORLY THE
NEXT TIME OUT,
REVIEW YOUR
FUNDAMENTALS OF
GRIP, STANCE, AIM,
AND BALL POSITION.

—Harvey Penick

FUNDAMENTAL #9

When in a Slump, Get Back to Basics

When in a Slump, Get Back to Basics

As a PGA instructor, Rick often is called on to help his students out of a slump. Unlike a teaching session in which he is explaining and demonstrating a new skill or position, when his regular students are struggling with their game, he observes their fundamentals in action. Looking for a faulty technique or bad habit they might have picked up, he watches them from start to finish: grip, posture, alignment, swing path, and body rotation.

Most of the time he can fix their swing and help them out of their slump by going back to the basics of their setup. If you already have a good knowledge of your swing but can't break out of a slump, Rick suggests these three steps:

1. Make one or two simple adjustments to bring back the good, natural feel that has been eluding you.
2. Review your own notes or videos from previous lessons.
3. Get a lesson from your instructor who already knows your swing and tendencies.

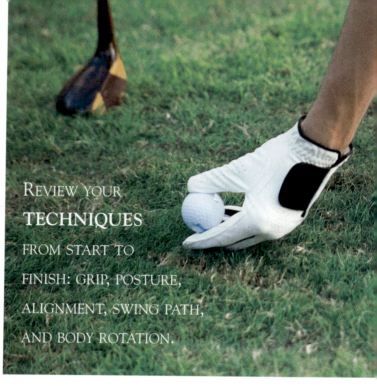

REVIEW YOUR **TECHNIQUES** FROM START TO FINISH: GRIP, POSTURE, ALIGNMENT, SWING PATH, AND BODY ROTATION.

provisional

1. a second chance, granted by a spouse, to do something well; must be humbly requested by the offending spouse; an admission that you've made a mistake and would like the opportunity to replay the situation

2. a second shot after the initial shot is considered lost; incurs a one-stroke penalty; player must ask permission to take a provisional

When in a Slump, Get Back to Basics

Fundamentals are especially helpful when a couple needs to break out of a slump.

We were recently paired in a foursome with two men. Early in the round, they bragged about taking regular golf lessons, owning the finest equipment, and playing golf as often as they could. Later in the round, Roger asked one of the men how long he had been married. "Less than a year," he answered matter-of-factly, "and our marriage is a mess."

"Have you seen a counselor together?" Roger asked.

"No!" he replied quickly, making clear that he saw counseling as a sign of weakness.

It's not uncommon to find people who are willing to spend plenty of time and money to improve their golf game but aren't willing to put even a fraction of that effort into improving their marriage. As in golf, however, marriage often requires making adjustments.

As a premarital and marriage counselor, Roger requires engaged couples to attend an eight-week counseling series that helps them establish a solid foundation for their marriage. He teaches the couple skills and methods to build and maintain a healthy marriage. These fundamentals are especially helpful when a couple needs to break out of a slump.

According to Roger, a healthy marriage relationship must be built upon some basic, immutable fundamentals:

1. Listen before you speak.
2. Don't go to bed angry.
3. Look for a solution that is win-win for both spouses.
4. Manage your anger.
5. Focus on your partner's strengths, not weaknesses.

As in golf, when your marriage is in a slump, getting back to the basics can create a spark of fun and love to keep moving you forward.

Wher

You will never even begin to score consistently
well until you know exactly how far you can
hit the ball with each club under
varying conditions.

Jack Nicklaus

from *Golf My Way*

ROUNDING THE TURN
Great Players Take Lessons

Becky played golf for many years using the same golf swing. As long as she muscled, adjusted, and compensated her way through a round of golf, she could maintain an acceptable score. But she never seemed to improve or have fun on the course. Her lack of enjoyment and consistency kept her from joining a league or getting a handicap.

Finally, she listened to her brother, Rick, who told her that she would never break through to measurable improvement until she learned good, basic fundamentals of the game: posture, grip, alignment, body rotation, and swing path.

Tired of mediocrity, she decided it was time to submit to changing her entire swing and take lessons. Rick's instruction included videotaping Becky's swing so she could see on tape what she was unable to feel. After a series of lessons, her first round of golf felt strangely unfamiliar. She simply could not find the feel of her more comfortable

Rounding the Turn

(but improper) old swing. To her surprise and disappointment, she scored even higher with her new swing!

Her second round of golf was even more frustrating. Becky had assumed that her lessons would result in immediate improvement on the course, but instead, her score kept rising. Noticeably discouraged, she decided to give up and return to her old way of manipulating a shot—but she couldn't find it anymore.

Rick challenged her again: "If you will commit to this and work on developing a feel for this new swing, your score will drop lower than you've ever scored before. It takes time, but a feel for a better swing path will come, and you'll gain a respect and recognition—even muscle memory—for the new swing."

So Becky began to practice and play more often. She reviewed her practice tapes and focused on developing the new feel and skills. Overcoming her pride, dealing with the strangeness of performing the new swing, and temporarily forfeiting a measure of success while making the transition was difficult; but she held on to the promise of becoming a better golfer.

Great Players Take Lessons

In six months, Becky had acquired a handicap and broken one hundred. She asked her brother to schedule her for lessons, lobbied for a new set of clubs, and begged her mother to play an extra eighteen holes with her once a week. As she set aside her previous patterns for the new methods, her game improved and she enjoyed the game far more than she ever had before.

Golf is both a mental and physical game. Encouragement, advice, and direction from a knowledgeable or respected friend, coach, or instructor will bring valuable perspective to the inevitable difficulties of the game. If you are experiencing recurring problems in your golf game, consider consulting your local PGA instructor.

Much like golf, marriage is multifaceted. To maintain a great relationship, you might need the help of a counselor, pastor, or mentor who can encourage you and tell you the truth. Don't hesitate to speak with a professional counselor, especially if you're struggling to master any of *The Front Nine* fundamentals. Work on your marriage with the same intensity you would use to improve your golf game, and you'll see measurable improvement.

To CONTACT the Tirabassis to speak at a couples conference or to host a *Front Nine* event, please call, e-mail, or write them at:

800-444-6189

www.thefrontnine.com

cyl@changeyourlifedaily.com

Change Your Life

Box 9672

Newport Beach, CA 92660